D1450625

Seals, Sea Lions, and Walruses

JUDITH HODGE

BARRON'S

CONTENTS

INTRODUCTION

Seals are some of the best-known animals of the oceans. They are found on sandy shores, rocky outcrops, ice floes, even tropical beaches. Seals live all around the world, but they are most common in the icy waters of the Arctic and Antarctic. This is probably because food supplies are better there than in warmer waters.

Much of a seal's time is spent in the sea chasing fish to eat. However, they do not live a completely aquatic life. Seals need to come ashore to give birth, molt (shed their fur), or just to rest. Nevertheless, they have adapted well to living in water.

Millions of years ago their ancestors lived on land. They began hunting in the oceans, and over time, seal bodies became more streamlined for swimming. Hands and feet developed into webbed flippers.

Another change to a watery way of life is the seal's thick layer of blubber, or fat. Like other mammals, they are warm-blooded. This means that the animal's body temperature stays quite high even in polar seas. To cope with the cold, seals have grown thick fur and a layer of blubber or fat to keep them warm.

Seals are mammals like whales and dolphins (and people). This means they have lungs, not gills like fish. Seals close their nostrils under water and have to surface to gulp fresh air. Some species can hold their breath for more than 30 minutes when diving.

Opposite: The monk seal is the only warm water seal and one of the rarest marine mammals in the world.

The massive elephant seal weighs in at more than 4 tons and grows to 21 feet. The smallest species, ringed and Baikal seals, still reach 4 1/2 feet and weigh 140 pounds.

DIFFERENT KINDS of SEALS

The scientific name for seals is "pinniped," a Latin word meaning wing- (or fin-) footed. This is a good description of the shape of a seal's flippers. There are 33 different species of pinniped: 18 true seals, 14 eared seals, and the walrus. True seals make up roughly 90 percent of the 50 million pinnipeds throughout the world today (30 million are crabeater seals from the Antarctic!).

You can guess the main difference between true seals and eared seals from their names. True seals have no obvious earflap but flat openings at the sides of their heads. Eared seals, a group made up of sea lions and fur seals, have tiny visible ears. Both types, however, have good hearing, as all seals have fully functioning ears below the skin's surface.

Swimming styles also vary among the

True seals have a round, chubby shape and no obvious ear flaps. With their thick layer of blubber they are better suited to life in an icy environment. Eared seals must keep moving in water, whereas true seals can float motionless without becoming chilled.

Everything is reversed on land. A true seal's front flippers cannot turn under its body, which makes it a clumsy mover: it has to wriggle and hunch to get along. Eared seals spend more time ashore than true seals. They use their strong front flippers to raise their bodies. This makes them more agile as they can walk on all four limbs.

Left: Eared seals use their back flippers as rudders to change direction. **Below:** The earflap of the eared seal, though tiny, can be clearly seen.

different kinds of seals. True seals are graceful swimmers, pushing through the water with their hind flippers pressed together to form a tail shape. Eared seals have longer flippers and use their strong front limbs like oars. The walrus swims using all four flippers.

TRUE SEALS: ANTARCTIC SEALS

Seals of the Antarctic include the crabeater seal, leopard seal, Weddell seal, and the Ross seal. Unlike the others, crabeaters feed mainly on krill, a tiny shrimplike creature. They take in mouthfuls of sea water, then filter out the krill through special teeth that act like a sieve. The large numbers of crabeater seals are probably due to a lack of competition for food.

Crabeaters are hunted by killer whales and leopard seals but often manage to escape, judging by marks on their pale fur. True seals are usually slow

Leopard seals, named for their distinctive markings, are the solitary predators of the Antarctic.

movers on land, but crabeaters can reach speeds of up to 15 mph.

Leopard seals are also fast on the ground, often slithering on ice more quickly than people can run. They are the killer whales of the seal world. Powerful, solitary animals, leopard seals roam the seas looking for things to eat. Penguins are their favorite food, but they will eat fish, squid, the rotting carcasses of whales, and even other seals.

With their distinctive coats of gray with pale spots, leopard seals are easy to identify. They are

Like most Antarctic seals, Weddell seals spend much of their time in the sea, which is the warmest place, especially in winter.

Crabeater seals are often called "white seals" because of their light coloring. The pups are born with thick brown fur, which gradually fades after molting.

very large, with males growing up to 11 feet long. Females are even longer—up to 20 inches more—which is unique among seal species.

Weddell seals are the same length but have stouter bodies. They are dark gray and covered with pale blotches. Weddell seals are the deepest divers among the seal species, going to depths of up to 2,000 feet to find fish and squid on the ocean floor.

Ross seals scour the sea floor for squid, octopus, cuttlefish, and shellfish. They are shy and clumsy out of water, but they can outswim a killer whale in the ocean.

NORTHERN or ARCTIC SEALS

There are many more ringed seals than any other species in the Arctic. It is the smallest of all seals, with both males and females measuring up to 7 feet.

The harp seal, ringed seal, and bearded seal are the three specialist seals of the Arctic. The scientific name for the harp seal means "ice-lover," and it often lives far out to sea on drifting pack ice. It is one of the most aquatic c all seals and a great traveler, moving south during winter to breed.

In contrast, the ringed seal dislikes the open ocean and prefers to stay near the coast. Ringed seals are named after their coats, which are covered with dark blotches circled with pale rings. The ribbon seal is another named after its appearance. With a coat of chocolate brown with white bands around the back, front flippers, and stomach, the ribbon seal has the most striking coloring of all seals.

The bearded seal has very bushy whiskers, more like a moustache than a beard, on either side of its snout. They are large seals, up to 9 feet in length, and are grayish-brown in color.

Hooded seals are also known as bladder-nosed seals. Both sexes have a black hood from above their eyes to their muzzle. The males also have a red bladder, which can be forced out of the left nostril like a balloon. This can be inflated either to show fear or anger or to attract a mate. Measuring up to 11 feet, hooded seals are the largest true seals in the Arctic region—all in all, they are hard to miss!

The harp seal's thick coat and layer of blubber ensure that it can survive the coldest of climates.

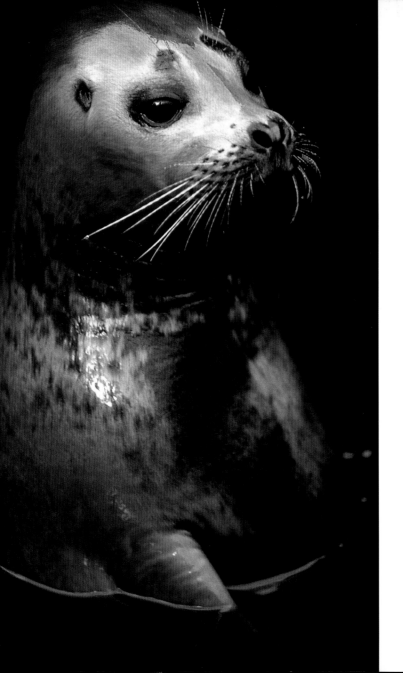

HARBOR or COMMON SEALS and GRAY SEALS

Harbor or common seals live in the slightly warmer waters of the North Atlantic and North Pacific where they feed on fish and octopus. They are among the most common seal species, though very shy. Skin tones among harbor seals range from dark gray to dull yellow covered with brown or black blotches. They are small and fat with more rounded heads than gray seals, with which they are often confused.

Many seals are great travelers, but harbor seals rarely venture more than 15 miles from where they were born. They spend more time on land than other seals, climbing onto rocky ledges or sandbanks to sleep during the day.

Harbor or common seals are preyed upon by killer whales and by large sharks in the Pacific Ocean. They also have a long history of being hunted by people.

Gray seals are sometimes seen in the same waters as harbor seals. They are much larger, with males up to 11 feet in length, and have longer muzzles than common seals. Females have pale skin with dark spots and the males have dark skin with light spots.

Gray seals will eat almost any type of food they can catch, usually fish, crustaceans, and

Gray seals are ideally colored to blend in with their rocky surroundings.

shellfish. They have long claws to help them climb on rocks but gray seals look clumsy on land. They are more at home in water and can even sleep in the shallows, bobbing to the top automatically to take another breath.

ELEPHANT SEALS

Above: Elephant seals enjoy basking in the sun on land, flicking sand over their bodies to cool themselves or ease itching caused by parasites and dry skin.

Elephant seals are giants among pinnipeds. The females look like any other seal, but the bulls weigh only slightly less than their namesake, the elephant. Some can be up to 20 feet long and weigh 4 tons. They also have a trunklike nose, which they fill with air and blow like a trumpet to frighten off rivals during the mating season.

People very rarely see elephant seals at sea because they spend most of their time diving, up to 60 times a day. They dive in deep waters for small sharks and rays, squid, and octopus, searching them out with their large eyes. Elephant seals can stay underwater for up to two hours by using oxygen stored in their blood. All seals can do this but elephant seals are the best at it.

Elephant seals are usually seen on land during molting, which takes about 40 days. During this time they have to stay out of water and take mud wallows, as the skin comes off in strips.

Elephant seals rear up on their back flippers when under threat. There is fierce fighting during the breeding season, when rival males rake each other's neck with their teeth.

There are two species of elephant seal. Both were hunted almost to extinction for their fat, which was used as lamp oil in the nineteenth century. The northern elephant seal, once common in the waters of southern California, was hunted until there were only 20 animals left. Numbers recovered from this remaining stock and today there are 125,000 animals breeding off the coasts of California and Mexico.

Southern elephant seals are larger than the northern species and found in greater numbers. They live on most islands of the southern oceans, preferring their homes to be ice-free.

Elephant seals are named after their trunklike noses, large size, and tough hide, which looks like elephant skin.

MONK SEALS

Monk seals get their name from their dull gray or brown color, like the color of cloaks worn by monks. They are the only seal specie that live all year round in warm water. Instead of toughing it out in the icy polar oceans, they spend thei days chasing fish in tropical seas and lying on sunny beaches.

Unfortunately, these are just the places that people like to visit. Monk seals are very shy animals and they have been badly affected by human invasion of their habitats. Tourism, fishing, and pollution have all taken their toll on monk seal numbers.

The Mediterranean monk seal once lived throughout the region from the Black Sea to the Moroccan coast. There may now be as few as 500 left, making it one of the world's

Scientists have found that monk seal mothers abandon their pups when they are disturbed or frightened, before the young are ready to fend for themselves.

most endangered mammals. Conservationists are working hard to protect the seals' remaining habitats by setting up nature reserves.

The Hawaiian monk seal is slightly smaller than the Mediterranean species. Its situation is also critical. There are only about 1,000 of the species left, most of them living in a wildlife sanctuary. Seal numbers dropped dramatically when the Hawaiian Islands were used by the United States military during World War II.

Unlike other seals, monk seals spend their time sunning themselves on beaches in warm climates.

The Caribbean monk seal is already thought to be extinct as there has not been a sighting since 1952.

EARED SEALS: FUR SEALS

(Northern, Australian, New Zealand, South American, Juan Fernandez, Galapagos, Subantarctic, Antarctic, Cape)

There are two groups of eared seals: the sea lions and the fur seals. The main difference between them is the fur seal's thick, silky underfur, much sought after by hunters. There are nine species of fur seals, all of which have been hunted for their fur. In contrast with most other endangered species, though, numbers of fur seals have risen quickly since hunting has been stopped or controlled.

The northern fur seal lives in the North Pacific Ocean and breeds in the Pribilof Islands of the Bering Sea. Males are dark brown, shading to gray at the shoulders. They reach about 6 1/2 feet in length. The females are gray and both sexes have pale fur on their chests.

Northern fur seals are noisy, outgoing animals, spending the days sleeping and hunting at night. As winter approaches they migrate south to California and Japan to find

Fur seals are smaller than sea lions but both groups have small external ears.

fish in warmer waters. They return in spring to the breeding grounds where the bulls gather harems of up to 40 cows.

Up to eight species of the southern fur seal are recognized, all of which look somewhat similar. They have more pointed snouts than their northern cousins, and all live in different places on the southern coasts of Africa, South

Below: In warm weather, fur seals hold their flippers out of the water to cool themselves.

The fur seal's coat has two layers of hair. Longer, thicker hairs protect the seal as it scrapes against the rocks. But it is air bubbles caught in the dense underfur that keep the seal warm.

America, Australia, New Zealand, and Antarctica. Their diet varies according to where they live, but it is mainly different types of fish, squid, and the occasional penguin. Only the Antarctic fur seal lives on a diet consisting primarily of krill.

17

SEA LIONS
(California, Steller's, Southern, Australian, Hooker's)

The five species of sea lion are easier to tell apart than the fur seals. Sea lions have a shaggy mane, which gives them their name. They have less underfur than fur seals and are larger in size.

The California sea lion, with its dark brown coat, is the species most often seen in zoos and circuses. The species makes some seasonal movements up and down the California coast, where it lives on rocky offshore islands. It prefers squid, octopus, and cuttlefish, but will eat fish, shellfish, and even seabirds.

You can tell the age of Australian sea lions by the patch of hair on their head and neck, which turns pale as they grow older. They have a restricted habitat around the Australian coastline and

California sea lions are intelligent and playful. They can learn tricks, particularly ones that show off their balancing skills.

Right: Fur color varies enormously among Australian sea lions, but they are usually pale brown with a yellowish tinge, and the head and neck are usually pale yellow.

Steller's sea lions have very sharp eyesight both in and out of water, and hunters used to have great difficulty getting within range.

number only about 10,000. There are similar numbers of Hooker's sea lions living on the subantarctic islands of New Zealand.

In contrast, the Southern sea lion population is more widespread, stretching around the coast of South America and in the Falkland Islands, where half the total population can be found. It is the most common sea lion. Adult males have a pale gold mane and reach 8 feet in length.

Steller's is the largest sea lion. Males grow to 11 feet long and have long manes around their muscular necks. Females weigh only about a third of the bull's weight. Both sexes have reddish-brown fur. The species lives in the North Pacific Ocean and feeds on squid and many different kinds of fish.

Steller's sea lions are great wanderers and swimmers, and are found all along the Alaskan coast and south to California. Unfortunately, their numbers are in decline and scientists are not sure why.

WALRUSES

The long white tusks of the walrus are unmistakable. These overgrown teeth were once thought to be used to rake the seabed for shellfish, especially clams and cockles that are the walruses' main food. It is now believed that the animal's fleshy snout is used for digging up prey. Tusks serve better as weapons in fighting and as hooks for hauling themselves onto land. Both males and females have them.

Of all the pinniped species, walruses are second only to elephant seals in size. They have thick wrinkly skin covered with coarse hair. Adult males start to go bald as they get older. But they keep their moustaches, which are made up of lots of very sensitive whiskers. These hairs are used to find food on the dark ocean floor and also to guide the shellfish into the mouth.

A group of walruses turn pink in the sun as the blood flow to their skin increases.

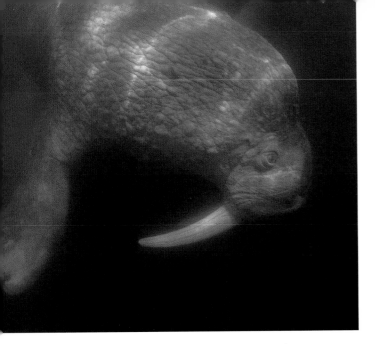

Above: Walruses look like overgrown sea lions and can move like eared seals using all four limbs. But they have no external ears, only a fold of skin marking the location of the ear. This puts them in their own family of pinnipeds.

The names of the two species of walrus, the Atlantic and Pacific, are misleading. Both populations are only found in the Arctic regions and the northern parts of both oceans. Walruses used to be more widespread, but hunting has greatly reduced their numbers. The Pacific animals are, on average, slightly larger with longer tusks.

The walrus is a very sociable, noisy animal. Large numbers gather together on rocky shores or ice floes to rest during the day. There is always one animal on guard, watching out for their greatest natural predator, the polar bear.

Below: Walruses are extremely fat! As much as half of their body weight is blubber and they have a tough, 2-inch-thick hide.

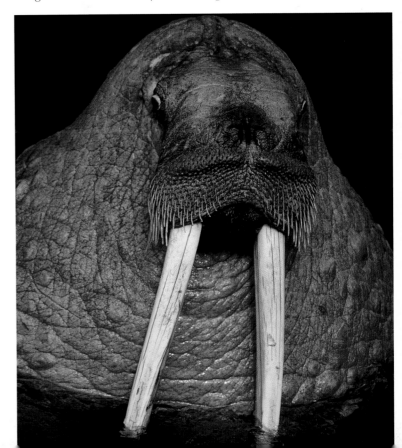

THE PINNIPED'S BODY

Seals have sleek, torpedo-shaped bodies and powerful flippers for moving swiftly through the water. True seals are the better swimmers, with a head that merges into the body with no obvious neck, for a more streamlined shape. They swim by moving their back flippers and tail from side to side. The front flippers are used to steer.

Eared seals have front-flipper drive. They swim with their large front flippers, using their rear flippers to steer. They are still very fast underwater.

Seal ancestors were once land dwellers and flippers were arms and legs. You can still see five claws on the end of a flipper. They now have

Above: Like dolphins, some seals "porpoise" leap out of water when they are swimming fast.

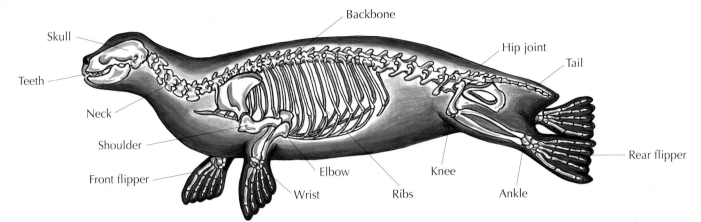

Skull

Teeth

Neck

Shoulder

Front flipper

Wrist

Backbone

Hip joint

Tail

Rear flipper

Elbow

Ribs

Knee

Ankle

webbed skin between the digits, which helps with swimming.

Pinnipeds often bask in the sun to warm up. But they are so well insulated that they can easily get too hot. When this happens they cool off by waving their front flippers in the air or burying them in the sand.

The thick covering of oily, waterproof hair all over their bodies stops the animals from losing some heat. But it is their blubber that really keeps them warm. Blubber also helps seals stay afloat and acts like a cushion when they move about on rocky ground.

Coloring varies between the different species of seal. Most have fur that is paler on the

underpart of their bodies than on the top. This is a form of camouflage, making it harder for their prey to see them in the water.

The seal's shape is streamlined to form an efficient swimming machine.

SENSES and COMMUNICATION

A seal has senses similar to a dog's, including a good sense of smell. A mother is able to recognize her pup by its scent in a crowded breeding colony. Seals also use their noses for sensing danger when resting on dry land.

All pinnipeds, apart from the walrus, can see well both in and out of water. Both eyes point forward—this is helpful for judging distances when chasing fast-moving prey.

An elephant seal puts his big hooter to good use during the mating season, puffing air into it to increase the volume of his roaring.

Right: With their large eyes, seals are thought to see as well underwater as a cat can on land.

But hearing is probably the seal's most important sense, even among earless seals.

Seals also have very strong, sensitive whiskers growing out of their cheeks. These are thought to pick up the smallest movements in the water, helping them to feel when fish or other creatures are nearby. Long whiskers are especially useful in dark or murky waters.

Pinnipeds are very vocal creatures. They communicate with each other through barks, grunts, and whistles. Quieter sounds, such as hissing and whining, are more frequently used as a threat. Males will make a noise to frighten off rivals, or a mother and her pup will bark to find each other.

Walruses have the loudest voices in the Arctic with a wide vocabulary of sounds. They bark, roar, and make a deep baying noise like large dogs. Seals that mate in water, like walruses, make noisy underwater sounds like a deep-sea bell. They will also rise out of the water to whistle, growl, and clack their teeth!

All seals have whiskers that are sensitive to movement in the water and help them hunt.

LIFE CYCLE

Most seal species live in groups and make long journeys together. But some, like the harp seal, are solitary species, only meeting in larger numbers at breeding grounds on ice, rocky islands, or beaches. These are known as rookeries and can hold up to 150,000 seals.

Male or bull seals often have several mates. They arrive first at the rookery to claim a space for themselves and any females they can attract. Male gray seals, elephant seals, eared seals, and walruses gather large harems of cows. The dominant bull, or beachmaster, sometimes has a harem of as many as 30–50 females.

Above: Newborn pups are born with their large eyes open. They are covered in a woolly birth coat of fur, which they molt for a sea-going pelt.

Females usually only produce one pup. They haul out of the water just before they give birth, though some, like the harbor seal, have their babies in shallow water. The ringed seal digs out a cozy igloo in the snow in which to give birth to its young and to protect them from the weather.

Like all mammals, seal pups live off their mother's milk for the first few weeks or months. Seal milk is very rich and creamy and the young put on weight quickly. Pups soon learn

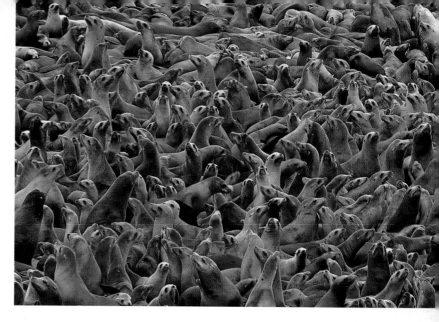

Breeding beaches are so crowded that pups are often crushed by huge males either fighting or rushing over to mate with females.

Below: The mother seal rolls over on her side as the pup nuzzles her, making it easier for the pup to suckle.

to swim and find their own food. Seal mothers vary in the amount of care they give their babies. Eared seals look after their pups for much longer than true seals.

Seals can survive for up to 30 years if they avoid their main enemies. They are social animals but family ties are not as strong as those among other sea mammals, such as whales. Walruses form some of the closest groupings, enjoying each other's company in close quarters on beaches.

HUNTERS and HUNTED

All seals are hunters, feeding on fish and other sea creatures such as squid and shellfish. They can outswim most animals, grabbing their slippery prey with spiky teeth. Seals will hold a fish between their front flippers, eating everything but its head.

Some pinnipeds eat a wide range of food while others have a more specialized diet. Leopard seals are skilled hunters and will eat almost anything that moves, from penguins to baby seals. Their long flippers help them change direction quickly when giving chase underwater.

Polar bears present the main danger for seals in the Arctic. The animals can creep up on sleeping seals and seize them with their sharp claws before the seals escape into the water. Polar bears will also lie in wait by the seals' breathing holes in the ice, waiting for them to

Seals are not only swift but also agile swimmers, twisting and turning sharply to pursue schools of fish.

surface. With their huge forepaws they lift the seal out onto the ice and then kill and eat it.

Seals rely on their swimming speed when being chased in the water. They can easily swim faster than polar bears, but may fall prey to killer whales. Even thick-skinned walruses are not safe—a pod of killer whales will surround a herd in the water and attack them. In warmer waters, pinnipeds are hunted by sharks.

Killer whales will sometimes launch themselves onto ice floes in an attempt to capture hapless seals.

SEALS and PEOPLE

Throughout history, humans in many parts of the world have hunted seals. The Inuit (Eskimo) people of the Arctic have always found a use for every part of the animal, from eating the meat to making clothes and kayaks from the skin. But whereas groups like the Inuit never killed many seals, commercial hunting did great damage to seal populations.

In the early 1700s whalers began to kill seals for profit, mainly for their coats but also for lamp oil. Walruses were the first seals to be hunted commercially. The ivory from their tusks was very valuable,

Above: There has been an outcry over the killing of snow white harp seal pups for their fur. Animal activists have sometimes sprayed the coats with dye to make them worthless to hunters.

and their tendency to gather in huge herds made them easy targets. In the southern oceans, millions of elephant and fur seals were killed.

Some hunting still takes place but there are now controls in place and the market for seal products is small. Some animals are still sought by commercial fishermen who claim that seals damage nets and cause shortages of fish stocks. Seals also face problems caused by pollution. The paper mills around Lake Baikal in Russia, for example, have poured highly poisonous chemicals into the lake, putting the Baikal seal on the endangered list.

The future for seals is a mixed one. Unlike whales, seal populations have mostly recovered and only the two species of monk seal are now in serious danger of becoming extinct. But other species are becoming rare, and some seal populations, such as the Steller's sea lion and the southern elephant seal, are getting smaller every year. The main problem is that seals are very sensitive to intrusion. The best action people can take is to leave them in peace.

Seals often get tangled in marine rubbish such as packing straps and nets. As the animal grows, its neck or flipper is cut by the plastic.

INDEX

First published in 1999 by David Bateman Ltd, 30 Tarndale Grove, Albany Business Park, Albany, Auckland, New Zealand

Copyright © David Bateman Ltd, 1999

First edition for the United States and Canada published by Barron's Educational Series, Inc., 1999

Text: Judith Hodge, B.A. (Hons)
Photographs: New Zealand Picture Library, Key-Light Image Library
Design: Errol McLeary

All inquiries should be addressed to:
Barron's Educational Series, Inc.
250 Wireless Boulevard
Hauppauge, NY 11788
http://www.barronseduc.com

International Standard Book No. 0-7641-1217-1

Library of Congress Cataloging-in-Publication Data
Walker-Hodge, Judith, 1963–
    Seals, sea lions, and walruses / Judith Hodge.
        p. cm. — (Animals of the oceans)
    ISBN 0-7641-1217-1
    1. Pinnipedia.   I. Title.   II. Series.
    QL737.P6W25 1999
    599.79—DC21   99-25183
                                                            CIP

Printed in Hong Kong
9 8 7 6 5 4 3 2 1